D0578913

WRITE LIKE A PRO™

WRITING
A
NARRATIVE

ROGER BEUTEL AND LAUREN SPENCER

rosen publishing's
rosen
central®

New York

Published in 2012 by The Rosen Publishing Group, Inc.
29 East 21st Street, New York, NY 10010

First Edition

Library of Congress Cataloging-in-Publication Data

Beutel, Roger.
Writing a narrative/Roger Beutel, Lauren Spencer.—1st ed.
    p. cm.—(Write like a pro)
Includes bibliographical references and index.
ISBN 978-1-4488-4683-2 (library binding)—
ISBN 978-1-4488-4689-4 (pbk.)—
ISBN 978-1-4488-4747-1 (6-pack)
1. Authorship—Juvenile literature. 2. Narration (Rhetoric)—
Juvenile literature. I. Spencer, Lauren. II. Title.
PN159.B47 2012
808'.02—dc22

                                                          2010051939

Manufactured in the United States of America

CPSIA Compliance Information: Batch #S11YA: For further information, contact Rosen Publishing, New York, New York, at 1-800-237-9932.

CONTENTS

INTRODUCTION

Everyone has a story to tell. Whether they're incidents that actually happened or ones that are complete fantasy, the stories that exist in our minds are begging to be set free. Releasing them from our imaginations and memories can be achieved through narrative writing, a form of storytelling that brings the audience into the author's world. The best narrative moments are often those in which readers find themselves nodding their heads and thinking, "I've been there," or "Wow, that sounds amazing,"

Try to set aside time every day—even just fifteen minutes—to let your imagination run wild and write whatever comes to mind. Later, some of these ideas can be shaped into a story.

since the story paints such a realistic picture of the experience.

Narrative writing opens the door of a situation and exposes the events inside. As with any creative writing, one's ability to show an event unfolding through the use of interesting details is crucial. This narrative art is achieved with the use of pacing, characterization, dialogue, and action. A narrative piece needs a strong foundation on which to construct its story.

In this book, we will examine all the elements needed to get the creative process moving. This includes choosing an idea, firming up the plot, and strengthening the narrative voice. Another topic we will discuss is the process of working with others on a final draft in order to achieve the best possible story. We will also explore various literary techniques and how they can enhance your writing when combined with basic story elements.

Narrative writing often allows the author to tell a tale by revisiting a scene out of his or her own life. Narratives can also take on a fictional viewpoint. Whatever the choice, a narrative tale is one that offers insight into the mind of an author and the heart of his or her story.

chapter 1
Gathering Narrative Details

I n narrative writing, an author has a chance to make his or her mark on the world by relating a story that only he or she can tell. Whether it comes from a personal experience or is one that the writer has imagined, the point of a narrative is to bring a subject to life. By using sensory details, the five W's and H (who, what, where, when, why, and how), and basic story structure, any subject can be made exciting.

A personal narrative is based on an event in the author's life. It is written in the first person, using the pronoun "I," because the event is being told from the author's point of view. Ideas for personal narratives can come from think- ing about places you've been, people you know

ESSENTIAL STEPS

Read various personal narratives and fictional stories and then think about the differences between these two types of narrative.

Brainstorm about various narrative topics to write about.

Gather ideas and information to support your choice of subjects.

or have known, and experiences that have affected your life.

Fictional narratives are stories that are made up. Sometimes an author will take a personal experience and fictionalize it by creating a character and enhancing his or her actions with details that never happened. Or the story might be one that the author has created based on something he or she has read, observed, or heard.

Whether personal or fictional, a narrative requires a clearly written beginning, middle, and end. As the writer, you are the narrator of the story. It is your responsibility to take the reader on a detailed journey so that he or she can truly experience what you're describing.

Brainstorming, Collecting Details, and Organizing Ideas

When it comes to topics for narratives, personal experiences are loaded with possibilities. Think about times when you just couldn't wait to share something that happened. Call up memories of an experience that helped you learn something or gave you a new perspective on a person, place, event, or thing.

Next, think of details that will make the incident believable for whomever is reading the story. If you need to refresh your memory, search through old notebooks, journals, or photo albums. Think about past vacations you might have had or the first time you experienced something that was especially important to you. Very often, conversations with others will also remind you of details that could turn out to be effective additions to your story.

Speaking with family members can help refresh memories of the past. These recollections can provide fruitful story material.

For fictional ideas, you can use the same methods you would use to write a piece about a personal experience, or you can look to alternative sources. Writers often keep a file of printouts and clippings from newspapers, magazines, Web sites, blogs, and other sources to draw inspiration for future writing projects.

Another great way to capture ideas is to carry a small notebook, index cards, or scrap paper around with you to jot down ideas for both personal and fictional narratives. These moments can range from odd or interesting things that you see around you, to something you've overheard. They are fragments of thoughts, rarely complete sentences. Things like "Man on the park bench dressed in a natty tweed suit and jaunty scarf but wearing two differently colored socks," or "A young woman hurrying to work carrying a white bakery bag and trailing the smell of strong coffee and fresh-baked doughnuts." Direct observations about life make writing colorful and truthful.

Recording interesting incidents will help you create engaging details for current stories or help inspire future ones. Intriguing details can appear out of nowhere and capture your imagination. Recording these moments is invaluable to your writing.

Narrowing Your Focus

To narrow your topic choices, make a list of options on a sheet of paper or on your computer. Examine them and pick one that holds the most promise for engaging sights, sounds, and details to sustain the story from beginning to end. The idea needs to be focused so that you're not attempting to cram too many thoughts into one piece. For example, a subject like "sightseeing adventures I've had" is too broad. Unless you are writing a lengthy memoir, a topic like

OBSERVING YOUR SURROUNDINGS

Grab a small notebook or note cards and head out to a local diner or coffee shop. Notice everything around you. Find a place to sit with a good view of the entire space and the sidewalk outside. Concentrate on your thoughts. Next, observe your surroundings for about five to ten minutes, just watching and listening to your environment. What do you see, hear, and smell? Can you hear customer conversations, waitresses sharing a joke, the skillet sizzling, the coffee percolating, the silverware clinking, the cups and saucers clattering? Can you see people eating and drinking or reading books or working on laptops? Can you see people passing by outside, huddled and bundled against the cold or wilting and sweating in the heat? Whatever the sights and sounds are, jot them down in your notebook.

Next, notice details that are more specific. What sort of art is on the walls? Does the kitchen gleam with stainless-steel appliances, or is every surface browned and yellowed by cooking grease? What sorts of pies are rotating in the pie case? What assortment of smells can you detect? What are the solitary diners doing while they eat? Are there couples there on dates? What is happening at the tables of larger groups? Any incidents and details you can notice are fair game. Practice free writing these observations for about fifteen minutes without stopping.

that one may prove to be overwhelming. However, you can always take a broad topic and whittle it down.

Instead of attempting to write about all of your experiences visiting cities over the years, focus only on a specific trip, a specific day, or even a single event during a specific visit. Concentrating on a more specific and narrow time period will help you focus the mood of your piece. By doing this, you will write about events with specificity and detail, grabbing your reader's attention with a highly unique and particular experience. Trimming your focus will also help you manage the content of your entire narrative.

A good way to organize your ideas is with a chart that maps who, what, where, when, why, and how regarding the main character and the situation unfolding. These five W's and H are the thread that weaves together the narrative structure and establishes the foundation of your story.

A SECOND LOOK

Do I have a clear focus for my narrative, whether it's based on personal experience or imagined?

Have I mapped out interesting details to include in my story?

Do I feel connected to my topic?

Am I ready to start writing?

Charting the Five W's and H

Using a computer spreadsheet program or simply a pen and paper, indicate your subject at the top of the sheet. Mark off six columns across the spreadsheet. Devote one column to each of your five W's and H. You are using the five W's and H to focus on and organize the following points regarding the story's main character: who the story is about; what is happening to the main character; when it happened; where the character is; and why the character is there. You can also add how the character arrived at this situation. Example:

The day I first fell in love with live theater

Who	What	When	Where	Why	How
Me and my aunt	The first professional play I saw in the city	One year ago	The Beckett Theatre	A birthday present from my aunt	Trains, subways, taxis, and feet
	The Plough and the Stars, by Sean O'Casey	On a frigid November evening	Downtown; a ninety-minute train ride from my home	My aunt lives in the city and invited me to celebrate my birthday with a weekend at her place	

Using Details Provided by Your Senses

You can use sensory elements to describe how all the characters look, sound, feel (emotionally and

Charting Your Senses

	Me	Aunt	Audience Members	Actors
Looks	Underdressed: ratty sweater, faded jeans, dingy sneakers	Black skirt; black sweater; black boots; black beret; long, flowing black hair	Fur coats; high heels; jewelry; gowns; suits and ties	Heavy pancake makeup; wigs; turn-of-the-last century peasant outfits
Sounds	Silent	Quiet, except for occasional bursts of snorting laughter	Some whispered conversations, isolated snoring and coughing, the occasional "Shush!"	Clear and sharp without quite being loud

			Some were restless, some left early, some fell asleep, some applauded politely, some cheered and stood at the end	Impossible to know; seemed to increasingly disappear into their characters' feelings; seemed genuinely joyful at the curtain call
Feels	Initially restless, then entertained, finally awed	Satisfied and pleased but not overwhelmed		
Smells	Peppermint gum	Wool and leather	Perfume, cologne	Too far away to tell

physically), and even smell. This will pave the way for your first draft by mapping out the cast of characters and the action involved.

Create a story map and fill in the characters and main setting of your story along the top. Include your sensory list down the left-hand side. Then fill in details wherever you are able. Complete this chart using first impressions and memories. Record as many details as you can, and remember, since this is your narrative story, there's no such thing as a wrong answer.

chapter 2

The First Draft: Shaping the Narrative

When writing a narrative piece, the point of view you use to engage the reader is very important. Point of view is the position, or slant, from which a story is told. If this is a personal narrative, it will be written from your perspective, using the first person "I" to explain the action. Example:

My train pulled into the downtown station. I grabbed my things and stepped onto the platform. I was bursting with excitement and wanted to bound up the stairs to the station's main concourse. But what seemed like thousands of other passengers jammed the stairwell. When I finally inched my way up, I nearly created a pileup at the top of the staircase as I stopped to marvel, openmouthed, at the vaulted ceiling hundreds of feet above me, painted to look like the constellation-spangled night sky. People streamed past me,

ESSENTIAL STEPS

Focus on the narrator's point of view.

Plan the structure of the piece.

Write the first draft.

some pushing and grumbling, others more polite. I snapped out of my reverie and saw my aunt waiting for me across the station.

For fictional narratives, there are some point-of-view choices.

Omniscient (all-knowing): The narrator describes the thoughts of all characters in the story. Example:

The crowds parted around Tom, who had frozen at the top of the stairs, dazzled by the grand station's painted ceiling. Some grumbled and growled, irritated by a gaping greenhorn gumming up their smooth exit. Others were more kindly, remembering their own first arrival at this train station. They murmured things to Tom when politely passing like, "Gorgeous, isn't it?" and "They don't make them like this anymore!" His waiting aunt watched him from across the station, moved by his undisguised awe.

Limited Omniscient: The narrator can only tell the thoughts and feelings of the main character. Example:

Tom's train pulled into the downtown station. He grabbed his things and stepped onto the platform. He was bursting with excitement and wanted to bound up the stairs to the station's main concourse. But what seemed like thousands of other passengers jammed the stairwell. When he finally inched his way up, he nearly created a pileup at the top of the staircase as he stopped to marvel, openmouthed, at the vaulted ceiling hundreds of feet above him, painted to look like the constellation-spangled night sky. Frozen on the spot, he dimly sensed a swirling tide of both vexation and goodwill eddying and flowing past. His waiting aunt watched him from across the station.

Camera View (objective): The narrator tells the story, but he or she doesn't share any thoughts or feelings about the characters. Example:

Tom's train pulled into the downtown station. He grabbed his things and stepped onto the platform. He climbed the stairs with several hundred other passengers and paused at the top. Staring upward at the concourse's painted ceiling, Tom stood still as his fellow passengers swarmed around and past him. His waiting aunt watched him from across the station.

Once a point of view is selected, it's time to look at how the events in the piece will fit together. In narrative writing, the basic elements of a story establish its foundation. While the location, characters, and central point of the piece have already been decided during the prewriting process, now is the time to fill out the action. Before you begin writing your first draft, try charting a plot guide to determine your path.

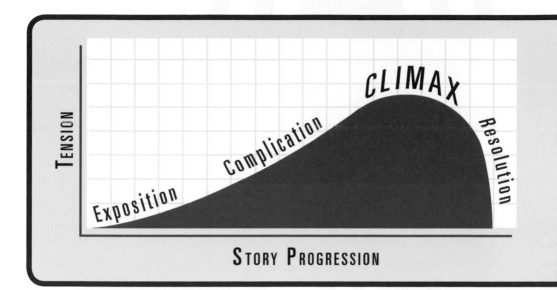

This story map charts the classic plot progression of a typical story, from setup (or exposition), to complication, through to climax and resolution. Notice how the narrative tension begins to rise when a plot complication is introduced and peaks at the climax.

A story map will launch you directly into your writing project. Don't worry about filling in every space or going in any particular order. Just let the ideas in your head loose onto the chart. Specific details will be filled in as your writing progresses. The purpose of this chart is to create an outline of your story's main points. Unless you are particularly fond of your title, you will now choose what is known as a working title. This temporary title is often revised before the final draft.

Plotline

Once you've established the setting, characters, and events in your narrative, you can examine various ways to present them so that your story flows from one moment to the next. This is called a plotline. It follows the action of your story. The plotline of any narrative has five parts: exposition (usually background information like the setting and characters); rising action (central part of the story that introduces the conflict); climax (the story's turning point); falling action (actions that lead to the story's ending); and resolution (the story's conclusion). Example:

My aunt and I arrived at the downtown theater and took our seats. The lights dimmed, and the red velvet curtain parted to reveal a cozy Irish drawing room. Fidgeting in my seat, I had trouble understanding the dialect and accents, and the big, stagy gestures felt artificial to me. I feared that this would be a long, boring, and uncomfortable evening. Then something amazing, almost magical, happened. The separation between the actors and me seemed to dissolve. I no longer was aware of sitting more than fifty feet away from the stage in the audience. I felt I was moving among the actors, who no longer seemed like actors but like real people, having real conversations, and caught up in genuine and overpowering emotions. I was no longer watching a performance. Instead, I was witnessing life lived fully and authentically all around me, just as the train passengers had swirled around me at the station, a human flow of conflicting emotions, all on display on that grand stage set of the vaulted concourse. I had fallen under the magical spell of live theater. I had discovered the secret—that theater IS life.

Other options for the order of your piece are chronological—explaining the event forward or backward in time—or physically from top to bottom or from bottom to top. Example:

Potential Plotlines:

Chronologically Forward:
I stood on the wind-whipped platform of the train station at Windsor Junction, collar of my overcoat turned up against the wind, a J. D. Salinger novel in my coat pocket, and a feeling of almost unbearable excitement rising in me. I was about to take a train into the city to meet my aunt, who was treating me to a weekend adventure for my birthday.

Chronologically Backward:
The actors appeared for their curtain call and bowed several times. Linked arm in arm, they then stepped back a few paces. The red velvet curtain came down, hiding them from our view. The music from the pit hit a crescendo and then stopped abruptly. The house lights went up. The audience stood blinking in the sudden quiet and brightness. The drama and comedy of real life had resumed. My life had been changed forever within the space of two hours.
I was not the same person who, fifteen hours ago and

seventy-five miles away, had woken up in Windsor Junction. The day had dawned back home breezy and brisk…

Physically from Top to Bottom:

The starry vaulted ceiling hundreds of feet above froze me in my tracks. Below it, the air was shot through with dust motes dancing in the sunlight, streaming through the train station's large, high windows. All around me people swarmed and rushed and pushed and shuffled. I saw my aunt looking for me across the concourse. Yet still my feet refused to move from the spot as I gazed up at the celestial ceiling.

Once you have decided on a vision for your narrative piece, begin writing your first draft. In order to maintain the flow of your work, don't stop writing unless you need to check your notes or examine your charts for details. Keep your words spilling onto the page as your story takes shape. Don't worry about its length or paragraph breaks, since you'll have a chance to shape it later. Keep the flow going until you feel the action is winding down. Don't worry about spelling or grammar now, since you will make those corrections later.

A SECOND LOOK

Have I included all the basic narrative elements in my story?

Is there a clear point of view and order to my writing?

Have I incorporated the information from my prewriting charts?

MAPPING YOUR STORY

A helpful way to gather details while developing your narrative's arc is to construct a story map. This can help flesh out and shape both nonfiction and fiction narratives.

Working Title: "The Theater Life for Me"

Setting: A city train station; fancy restaurant; downtown theater

Characters: Me, my aunt, train passengers, theater audience, actors

Problem: Initial inability to appreciate, be entertained by, or be inspired by a live play

Event 1: After arriving at the station, I was astonished and awed by the beauty and grandeur of the concourse and by the thousands of people bustling all around me.

Event 2: I met my aunt on the other side of the station, and we exited onto the street, where I caught my first

glimpse of the city's glittering canyons of steel and its river of people. We walked for an hour, with my aunt pointing out the sights and her favorite haunts.

Event 3: We arrived at my aunt's favorite downtown restaurant, full of excited and chattering "theater folk"—people who were either about to see a show or actors unwinding after a matinee performance. Over pretheater dinner, my aunt tried to explain why she loves going to see plays and what makes the theater experience so rare and pleasurable.

Event 4: We arrived at the theater, the show started, and I felt fidgety with boredom, skepticism, and incomprehension. I began to fear that I would not feel the magic that my aunt described, and I worried about disappointing her.

Solution: At the point of despair, I stopped trying so hard to enjoy myself or "get it," and suddenly the play began talking to me and I got lost in the performances, which no longer felt like performances but like real life unfolding before and around me. The actions on stage felt like real life, and the life of the city outside—on the streets, in the restaurant, in the train station—seemed like high drama and comedy on the grandest of stages.

chapter 3

Developing Your Characters Through Figures of Speech and Dialogue

Now that the first version of your narrative is drafted, it's a good time to notice where additional details can be added to give the piece more style. Describe your setting and characters by using the five senses. Examine your writing and find areas where information that electrifies the senses—such as sight, sound, touch, smell, and taste—can be added. This will add details that are unique to your story.

Figures of speech are writing techniques that form "word pictures." They are a great way to "show" an element in a story. One example of a figure of speech is hyperbole, which is the use of exaggeration. Hyperbole is used to stretch an element of truth in order to add extra emphasis to the message. In the following example, a fictional character narrates a

ESSENTIAL STEPS

Support your story with descriptive and sensory details.

Use stylistic elements that will engage the reader.

Fine-tune character descriptions.

moment following a long-distance track race in which the exaggeration is built on the truth that she is thirsty. Example:

No sooner did Suzanne break the winner's tape and cross the finish line than she headed straight for the water fountain. The time to celebrate would come later; right now, she was so thirsty, she could drink the ocean dry.

Another figure of speech is personification, in which something that is not human is brought to life. This technique adds an imaginative twist to narrative stories. Example:

When she reached the water fountain, Suzanne was dis-mayed to find it out of order. Like a desert hermit hoarding his precious supply of water, this fountain wasn't giving up any of its life-sustaining liquid.

Dialogue: Capturing the Sound and Rhythm of Actual Speech

The conversation between characters in stories is called dialogue. Quotation marks are used to set this dialogue apart from the rest of the text. Quoted speech adds another dimension to narrative writing by allowing the characters to speak for themselves. Unless it is neces-sary that you quote a long speech word for word, it's best to keep dialogue limited to a few sentences. Using dialogue in this way allows the story to have momentum. Dialogue should be just long enough to add a layer of detail. If a quoted passage lasts for too long, it usually sounds unrealistic.

Reading plays can be a great way to get a feel for how to write compelling, convincing, and artful dialogue.

Although people often say, "Write like you speak," this message has to do with an author's ability to bring his or her individual personality to the writing. If you listen to yourself or others during conversations, you will notice pauses and slang words. You only want to include these elements in your written work in moderation. In most cases, they are used only to fill out a character description. If dialogue too closely mimics real-life conversation, it sounds clunky and halting. Example:

Actual conversation:
"Hey...uh...did ya hear about how the...whatchamacallit...the water fountain got messed up down there, like by the track or whatever?" asked my brother.

Narrative text:
"Hey, did you hear that the water fountain near the track was vandalized?" asked my brother.

Always remember to set off spoken dialogue with quotation marks, which surround the exact words of the speaker. Example:

Suzanne said to her teammate, Casey, who was walking by, "Hey, what's the deal with the water fountain?" Casey replied, "Dunno. Looks like it was vandalized. The one in the gym still works; I just tried it." "Thanks," Suzanne replied. She tried to lick her dry lips, but her tongue felt too thick and parched to budge. "I would like to get my hands on whoever busted that water fountain. Is a lousy sip of water after a race too much to ask?!"

If you want to capture the essence of what someone has said without using his or her exact words, you can paraphrase. This means you can eliminate the need for quotation marks by reworking a spoken passage in your own words. Example:

Suzanne asked her teammate, Casey, who was walking by, what had happened to the water fountain. Casey didn't know, but suggested she use the one in the gym instead. Suzanne thanked her. Still thirsty and dry-mouthed, she fumed when thinking about whoever had vandalized the fountain.

Character Development

A deeper sense of your characters will develop when you open a window into their minds. Character development also brings texture to whatever incident is unfolding. There are a few different ways to write about a character's thoughts. This is called inner dialogue because it's as if the character were talking to himself or herself. Such reflection about a situation can bring the reader closer to a character's feelings. Example:

Suzanne headed to the gym, all excitement over her victory ebbing away as she thought about the vandalized water fountain and what would possess someone to do that. One person's selfish desire to wreck school property or get kicks ruins the environment for everyone else and makes the innocent suffer. It poisons the well. When Suzanne finally reached the gym and went in to drink at the fountain, she couldn't even savor the relief of quenching her thirst. She had become too filled with anger, her stomach too sour with disgust.

Another way to express inner feelings about your characters is through flashbacks, which call up memories as a reminder of something that's happened earlier. Example:

Suzanne was reminded of a time in kindergarten, when, for show-and-tell, she brought in her prized possession—a

The more literature you read, the more story ideas you will gain and the better your own writing will be.

snow globe that contained within it the Empire State Building and the Manhattan skyline. She was inconsolable when Derek Sharples, filled with either envy or simply a love of destruction, grabbed the snow globe from her hands and smashed it on the ground. Suzanne still felt heartbroken when she remembered that, and the vandalizing of the water fountain struck her as an equally senseless, stupid, and mean-spirited act.

Flash forwarding anticipates possibilities about how a situation could unfold based on the thoughts of the character. Example:

Suzanne wondered if this act of vandalism was part of a new trend. Were more and more things going to be broken and defaced in and around school? Suzanne was filled with horrible visions of broken computers, smashed windows, slashed tires, and graffiti-covered walls. Would students become afraid to walk the grounds or use the bathrooms and locker rooms? Would students become afraid to go to school at all?

Foreshadowing serves as a warning about something that will happen later in the story. It is like dropping a clue about a future event. Example:

When Suzanne arrived at the track, she briefly wondered why so many of her teammates were carrying water bottles from the gym. She was soon distracted, however, by the sight of her chief opponent, Dawn Ruggels, the county record holder, emerging from the visitor's bus.

Inner dialogue can also take the form of a conversation inside one character's head as he or she explores all the possibilities of the moment. Quotation marks are used for the main thought as if it's being said out loud. Example:

This vandalism had to be stopped before it got out of hand. "I'm going to do something about this," Suzanne vowed to herself. Maybe she would organize a school cleanup day or a school watch program. First thing tomorrow, she'd speak to the principal to pitch ideas and then call a special meeting of the student council. She knew some of her fellow students would mock her for her concern and vigilance. But I'm not about to let our school go downhill because of the actions of a few bad apples!

You'll be surprised by how much information you can relate to the reader by using inner dialogue.

A SECOND LOOK

Am I ready to revise my piece by adding figurative language?

Do I fully understand the use of quotation marks so that I can add dialogue to my narrative?

Am I willing to go to the core of the character's feelings in order to add depth to my story?

chapter 4

Revising Your Narrative

T he act of revision is so much more than merely correcting your spelling and grammar mistakes. Although those tasks are a part of the final preparation before your story can be shared, there are other essential steps to take first. These involve revising and polishing the details of your story. The word "revise" comes from the French word *réviser*, which means "to look at again."

This process of observation is where you, the author, examine your writing with a critical eye. This is the time to figure out what can be added or changed to make the piece more interesting.

As you begin this process, have your first draft and any notes or charts you've compiled handy. During your revision, you will have a chance to incorporate stylistic

ESSENTIAL STEPS

Identify areas that need elaboration and detail.

Improve the flow of your writing, its transitions, and sentence structure.

Rewrite your draft incorporating all revisions.

techniques for character and plot development examined in the previous chapters. Get focused and read through what you've accomplished while making changes directly in the story.

One thing that will hopefully shine through is the distinct style of your piece. This is called the "author's voice." If you feel that the first draft doesn't quite communicate your individuality, now is the time to improve it.

Personal computers and word processing programs have made revising and editing one's work fast and comparatively easy.

Structuring Your Sentences

The way sentences are formed also adds to the tone and flow of writing. A sentence is the vehicle that moves the story along with a smooth motion. By merging sentences in engaging ways, an author achieves a more fluid and interesting story.

A compound sentence is formed when two independent clauses, or single sentences that stand on their own, come together. You can also join related sentences by using punctuation, such as a semicolon.

Example:

Ms. Campbell's office was large and spacious; it had floor-to-ceiling windows on three sides.

Or a conjunction—words like "and," "or," and "but"—can be used. Example:

Ms. Campbell's office was large and spacious, and it had floor-to-ceiling windows on three sides.

Complex Sentences: Linking Up Clauses

An incomplete sentence that makes a statement is known as a dependent clause. It needs to link up with a complete sentence in order to be whole. When you put them together, they form a complex sentence.

Dependent clauses can begin with a relative pronoun like "who," "that," or "which." Example:

Ms. Campbell's smile, which was warm and friendly, put me at ease right away.

The sentence could have stood alone as:

Ms. Campbell's smile put me at ease right away.

PROOFREADING SYMBOLS

When you or someone else is correcting your piece, here are the symbols that should be used to give instructions for corrections:

∧	Insert letters, words, or sentences
ℓ	Delete
⌃	Insert a comma
⌄	Apostrophe or single quotation mark
⌄⌄	Double quotation marks
∿	Transpose elements (switch the order)
#	Insert a space
⌒	Close up this space
⊙	Use a period here
¶	Begin new paragraph
no ¶	No paragraph

But adding the dependent clause—"which was warm and friendly"—gives the sentence more detail and helps explain why the speaker begins to feel more relaxed.

A complex sentence can also use a subordinate conjunction to bring together independent and dependent clauses. These are used at the beginning of a dependent clause and can describe a detail about time (after, before, until), cause and effect (because, since, even, though), or a difference between two events (although, while, unless). Example:

After the interview was over, Ms. Campbell showed me out of the office, shook my hand, and said she'd enjoyed meeting me and would be in touch soon.

In this case, the word "after" sets up cause and effect. Read the following example of a revised draft. In doing so, notice how the author uses a variety of sentence types and lengths. Also, note the rhythm of the writing and its transitional words and phrases.

Document1

I should have known that this was the right place for me. The big band sounds of Duke Ellington played over the speakers, not the typical waiting room Muzak. The waiting room smelled like cinnamon and oranges. A comforting, reassuring smell. I was about to interview for

Page 1   Sec 1   1/1   At 1"   Ln 1   Col 1   0/0   ○REC ○TRK ○EXT ○OVR my first after-school job, and I needed all the reassurance I could get.

I was so nervous, I thought it was entirely possible I'd have a heart attack right there in the waiting room. My palms were sweaty. My pulse was racing. My mouth felt dry. The mint gum I was chewing obsessively had long since lost its flavor, leaving only a sour taste on my tongue. The agitated blood was rushing in my ears, sounding like the relentless crashing of an incoming tide. I wondered if it was too late to sneak away. But I had already given my name to the receptionist, so, for better or worse, I was committed. Time seemed to slow and stretch as I waited, like a sticky length of salt water taffy being pulled on a hot summer boardwalk. The last time I felt this nervous and anxious was when I was six years old and waiting in the doctor's office for a flu shot.

Finally, the office door opened and a well-dressed woman—my future boss?—called my name.

"John Murphy? Hello. I'm Catherine Campbell. It's nice to meet you. Come on in."

"Hiyesthankyouhello," I squeaked.

The office was large and spacious. It had floor-to-ceiling windows on three sides, looking out over the nearby park and the city streets beyond. Ms. Campbell asked me to take the seat in front of her desk. We settled into our seats, and I began nervously shuffling my résumé and references. "Don't blow this. Don't blow this. Don't blow this," I repeated to myself in a panic.

After a moment, I nervously glanced up at Ms. Campbell. Her smile, which was warm and friendly, put me at ease right away. All the tension melted away, and I found myself speaking easily (and in a normal pitch) about my interest in the job, my unique qualifications, and my relevant experience. Though time had oozed more slowly than molasses in winter in the waiting room, it now hurtled forward in a blur. After what seemed like only two minutes of my motormouthing, Ms. Campbell looked at her watch and announced that it was five o'clock. I had been in her office talking to her for more than an hour!

Rising from her desk and signaling that the interview had come to a close, Ms. Campbell showed me out of the office. At the door, she shook my hand.

"It's been such a pleasure to meet you. I really enjoyed our talk. I'll be in touch soon."

I wasn't sure if I had blown the interview by talking too much. I strained to remember exactly what had happened in there and what had been said. I hoped that I had let her get a word in edgewise. But her warm and genuine smile at our parting seemed to indicate that she had truly enjoyed our conversation.

I only had to wait one day to learn how the interview had actually gone. Ms. Campbell called me the next afternoon, reiterated how much she had enjoyed meeting me and discussing the job, and…asked me to report for work next Monday afternoon at 4:00 PM sharp! Despite both my paralyzing anxiety and manic blathering, I got the job!

This example of a revised draft makes use of many stylistic elements. Note its use of the five senses, hyperbole, flashback, foreshadowing, slow motion, and dialogue (both inner and outer) using quotation marks. Notice that when dialogue is used, a new paragraph is started for each character's quotation. Now examine your revised draft for the same elements.

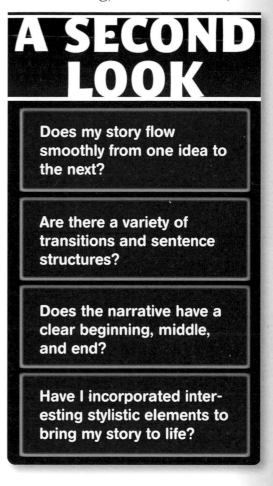

A SECOND LOOK

Does my story flow smoothly from one idea to the next?

Are there a variety of transitions and sentence structures?

Does the narrative have a clear beginning, middle, and end?

Have I incorporated interesting stylistic elements to bring my story to life?

chapter 5

The Final Polish

Your narrative piece is now in its final stages. Not only have you supported or increased the action by using various writing techniques, you've also brought out the best in the story by using your distinctive author's voice. Now you will have the chance to proofread and edit your piece by making spelling and punctuation corrections, getting opinions from your peers, and incorporating final changes into your work.

Start with spelling. If you have written your narrative piece on a computer, engage the spell-check option and correct any mistakes. If you've written your narrative in longhand, pull out a dictionary to look up any words that you're not sure about. If you have any doubts about a word, look it up.

ESSENTIAL STEPS

Complete a spelling and punctuation check. Add a final title.

Polish the story through group effort and constructive feedback.

Put the story into its final form.

The Final Stages

Giving your story an appropriate title is important in

order to grab the reader's attention. Think about other titles that make you curious. Why do you take notice of them? Does the title convey a sense of action? Does it speak about something you relate to? Consider these elements when revising a title for your story. Look over your narrative and think about its messages. The tone of your writing will give you an idea of what would best represent your piece, whether your story is suspenseful, dramatic, or anything else.

You don't want to give everything away, but you do want to deliver a promise about what the reader will find inside the story so that he or she will read on. Example:

> "My First Junior High Dance" (working title)
> "Dancing in the Dark" (drama)
> "Busting Moves and Breaking Ice" (comedic)

It's helpful to read your piece to another person at this stage. Often writers become so involved in their work that it becomes difficult to step outside themselves and see what might be missing or overdone. Meeting with your peers can give you an objective, outsider's perspective.

To ensure that your narrative has an interesting mix of elements, find a partner and trade your writing with him or her. Take four colored markers, each representing a narrative component: red for action; green for dialogue; black for physical descriptions of characters and setting; and blue for inner thoughts, observations, and feelings. Read your partner's work and use the markers to underline items in each sentence.

Once you're finished, return each other's narrative. If you see a rainbow of colors, you'll know your piece is balanced. But if you notice that one or more colors are barely used, review your story. Reread it to see how you can add more of those ingredients. Ask questions about your own piece and that of your partner. Think of at least one thing to say to compliment your partner's story.

Document1

New Steps to an Old Dance

I approached the school gym with dread. This sense of impending doom was heightened by the sheer disorienting strangeness of being at school and in those hallways after dark, on a Friday night. It was the night of my first junior high dance, and I would have preferred to have all my teeth pulled—without novocaine—to walking through those gym doors.

Page 1   Sec 1   1/1   At 1"   Ln 1   Col 1   0/0   ○REC ○TRK ○EXT ○OVR

Document1

My mom had forced me to attend the dance. We had moved to town over the summer, and in the first two months of school I still hadn't made any friends. This didn't bother me much. I'm a solitary person by nature and like to be by myself more often than not. But someone to pal around with once in a while would be nice. I was convinced, however, that I wasn't going to find that person at this dance.

My worst fears were realized when I entered the gym. First of all, it was really dark, and I stumbled into several classmates. Great. I'm sure everyone is thinking, "Hey, isn't that the weird new girl? Is she trying to slam dance?!" Once my eyes adjusted to the dim light, I saw that all the boys were lined up against one wall and all the girls against another. Never the twain shall meet, apparently. The boys were pushing and wrestling with each other, and the girls were clustered in select little groups. There was no group I could try to insert myself into; no one knew me well enough even for a casual, "Hello."

I was stranded between the two camps, incapable of joining either one, unable to take anonymous cover within any of the wrestling or chattering cliques. Suddenly the DJ began playing one of my favorite songs from a couple of years ago. My friend Wendy and I used to dance to it in my living room. Something about hearing that song again filled me with emotion and gave me courage. "I came to a dance, and darn it, I'm going to dance!"

Page 1   Sec 1   1/1   At 1"   0/0   ○REC ○TRK ○EXT ○OVR

The next thing I knew, I was striding into the middle of the deserted dance floor. I could feel a sudden hush and stillness from both the boys' and girls' camps, and all eyes turned toward me. I'm pretty sure I heard some snickering and hissing whispers. I paused in the middle of the floor, made a few tentative, jerky dance moves, trying to find the beat. Soon, though, the song's familiar strains drew me into a private reverie, and I was again that girl gleefully dancing with my good friend.

I don't know how long I was flailing around out there by myself, but at some point I opened my eyes and was startled to see dozens of people surrounding me. "Are they going to pick a fight? Are they going to mock me?" But no, they were clapping and smiling and cheering me on. Soon, several girls joined me, and, as we danced together, some boys shyly joined in while others pogoed and pushed and shoved on the margins.

Sadly, the song had to come to an end at some point. But when it did, one girl lingered by my side, tapped my arm, and said, "Hi. I'm Margaret. You're a really great dancer. You dance like you don't care what anyone thinks. I love that!" And, just like that, I had made a new friend and gained a new dance partner!

Creating a Supportive Community of Writers

It can be very intimidating to share your writing with classmates, peers, friends, or adults. That's why it's so important to understand how others often feel in the same position. With this in mind, here are some tips for how to use "constructive criticism" in order to help other writers.

Whether the author is reading in front of the class or sharing his or her piece with you directly, pay close attention to what he or she says. Do not yawn or fidget. Look at the author while he or she is speaking, or if you are reading the piece to yourself, read it carefully.

Write down questions you may have about anything that is confusing to you. Be very mindful of how you phrase your question. Instead of: "Your first sentence didn't make any sense," rephrase it to be more

A SECOND LOOK

Have I incorporated all the changes to make my piece better?

Am I ready to present my piece to others?

Have I included a final title that catches readers' interest?

Though it may seem intimidating at first, reading your work out loud to a group of fellow writers can be a highly rewarding experience. Allow yourself and your work to benefit from the valuable insights and constructive feedback of your peers.

helpful: "I was confused by the first sentence because I didn't understand where the action was taking place." As the phrase implies, your purpose is to be "constructive" by offering helpful ideas to other writers, just as you'd like them to do for you.

chapter 6

Sharing Your Work in Print, Online, and Out Loud

Writing is a very independent and imaginative activity. Through perseverance, revision, and a clear vision of what you want to achieve, you've brought your piece to a final stage. This is a moment worthy of congratulations! Now you can think about sharing your work with a wider audience.

Putting It Out There

Beyond your immediate circle, there exists a whole community of people who might enjoy reading what you've written.

Since narratives focus on storytelling, they are fun to read out loud and listen to. Think about presenting your work at a live reading with friends.

ESSENTIAL STEPS

Is your handwriting or font clear and easy to read?

Is your story printed or written on clean paper?

Are your title and author name visible?

Are your graphics clear and do they add to, and not distract from, your story?

To organize a reading, all you need is an appropriate space that is quiet and comfortable.

Digital Opportunities to Share Your Work

It used to be that in order to share your writing with a wider audience, you had to send the manuscript off to a publisher, who received hundreds of similar submissions a week. A very small percentage of these submissions would find their way into print. After many weeks of waiting and hoping, the author would often receive a short and curt rejection letter. Only a very few lucky and extremely talented writers were able to get their work published and read by the general public.

Today, however, the Internet has made it easy to post and share one's work with a wide audience and receive immediate feedback. There are many reputable Web sites—some of them the electronic versions of traditional publications—that invite and post user contributions, including fiction and narrative nonfiction.

An important online venue for narrative nonfiction is the Web site Daily Kos. This political and issue-driven Web site, which bills itself as an online

HOW TO ORGANIZE THE PERFECT READING

- Gather a small group to read—no more than ten readers at first. This will provide a less threatening atmosphere and help you build confidence.

- Find a space that is quiet and has comfortable seating. Readings can be held in people's homes, backyards, and even parks. But for places like libraries or coffee shops, you need to obtain permission in advance.

- Decide on a time limit for the readings. Each author should have an equal amount of time (between five and ten minutes is recommended).

- Create and distribute homemade invitations for the event stating who, what, when, and where.

political community, news organization, and activist hub, features articles written by permanent staff members, as well as guest pieces written by prominent politicians. Yet through the Daily Kos Diaries section, any visitor may post his or her narrative writing. Visitors can even create their own Web page within Daily Kos that features their archive of "diary entries." If a particular entry gets a lot of favorable feedback from readers or catches the eye of a staffer, it may be selected by the site's editors for prominent placement on the site's home page.

Online literary magazines are another superb venue for sharing your writing. *Amazing Kids!*, *Midlink*, *Merlyn's Pen*, *Skipping Stones*, *Stone Soup*, *Teen Ink*, and *Teen Voices* are all online literary magazines that welcome submissions from young writers. Even journals intended for older readers often welcome submissions from teen authors. One of the most prominent and dynamic of these is *McSweeney's*, a print and Web journal with a well-deserved reputation for championing fresh, daring, and offbeat writing from young and undiscovered writers. In addition, many publications and organizations sponsor writing contests for teens. These include the Alliance for Young Artists & Writers (which sponsors the Scholastic Art & Writing Awards), the National Council of Teachers of English, and *Weekly Reader*.

There are lots of online magazines and literary journals that invite submissions from teen authors, including the highly respected *Stone Soup* (http://www.stonesoup.com).

A fascinating phenomenon that has emerged in the Internet era is "fan fiction." These are stories that are written by fans of certain novels, films, cartoons, comics, graphic novels, plays, TV shows, and computer games. The fans use the original creator's characters to devise their own variations or extensions of the original story. For example, the HarryPotterFanFiction Web site contains over sixty-five thousand stories written by users. Works of fan fiction aren't usually endorsed by the original creators or publishers, and for this reason fan fiction itself rarely gets published. Yet fan fiction enjoys a vibrant life online, with an enthusiastic community of readers and fellow writers providing feedback, encouragement, and spurs to further creativity. Communities of fan authors can even get together and collaborate on stories. One of the leading venues for fan fiction writing is FanFiction.net.

Another way to share your narrative writing electronically is to create your own blog. While most people associate blogs with opinion and issue-based writing, they can also be appealing venues for narrative fiction and nonfiction. Web sites like LiveJournal, WordPress, and Blogger allow users to post journal entries online, share them with friends and other users, and create communities whose users can post group journals. The appearance of these journals can be customized, and photos and illustrations can be imported to enhance entries. Users can solicit comments from readers, creating a constructive dialogue between author and reader.

The Importance of Netiquette

The Internet has made it easy to post and share one's work with a wide audience and receive immediate feedback. This is an exciting development. Yet it also comes with some drawbacks and dangers.

You must be prepared for criticism, some of it fair and constructive, some harsh, and some just plain mean and abusive. If you receive a harsh or abusive comment or review, do not respond in kind. Things can escalate and get out of control very quickly, and you may become banned from the site. It's best not to respond at all. If you feel the person who has left a comment has crossed the line of decency, report that person to the site's webmaster. Do not get drawn into a war of words. And never write a comment about someone else's work that you would not want to receive yourself.

Engaging an abusive critic online can quickly open the door to harassment, cyberbullying, and flaming. The best way to stop the problem is to address it directly and do something about it. Report the cyberbully to the webmaster and do not continue to communicate with the bully. It is important to involve a trusted adult in the problem.

People often engage in flaming on blogs, chat rooms, message boards, or other sites where people are invited to post reviews of someone's writings. Strangers can get into arguments in these discussion threads, with an unlimited number of people able to view them. Sometimes, once one aggressive user attacks someone who has posted a comment he or she disagrees with, other users feel emboldened to join in and gang up on the flaming victim. This kind of cyber-bullying poisons what should be a supportive and stimulating environment.

Just as you do not want your writing to be savaged and do not want to be the victim of flaming, you must never attack someone online. Do not hide behind the idea that what you are posting is anonymous because people do not know you or your real name. Think about what you are posting. Would you be willing to deliver this message to the person face-to-face? Think about whether the statement you are posting is something you would like to read about yourself. Just think of what it would be like for all of your friends, family, classmates, and acquaintances to read unflattering things about you on your personal page or in the comments section of a posting.

Copyrighting Your Work

Copyright is a form of intellectual property law that protects original creative works, including literary, dramatic, musical, and artistic material, such as poetry, novels, movies, songs, computer software, and architecture. Copyright covers both published and unpublished works.

Current copyright law protects any work you create that is tangible and can be viewed or read either directly or with the aid of a machine or device. You do not have to register for a copyright to receive copyright protection; it is conferred automatically at the work's creation. Yet many people wish to register for a copyright in order to obtain a public record of the copyright and enable them to sue anyone who uses their work without permission.

You should be aware that when you post your writing to a Web site, in most cases you are surrendering your copyright to that site. The Web site retains the right to use your material as it sees fit without your further permission. It can even publish and distribute your material without your agreement and without reimbursement.

You should always read the Web site's terms of use, user agreement, submission guidelines, and other policies before posting your work in order to determine if you are surrendering your copyright and what the site may do with your work. You must also follow the site's rules about proper etiquette and guidelines concerning proper and improper content.

If you wish to post and share your work but retain the copyright, consider creating your own blog that you can control. Even on your own blog, however, you must not violate someone else's copyright by using their material—photos, video clips, extended quotes—without permission.

Get Writing!

If you're interested in creative and narrative writing, try to set aside time for writing every day. It need only be fifteen minutes. The important thing is to sit down and do it, regularly and often. Don't wait for inspiration to strike—just write! Consider joining author groups and writing workshops, whether they meet in person or online. And always be on the look-out for new material and interesting details. They may form the basis of your next masterpiece!

A SECOND LOOK

Does my narrative look interesting and pleasing to the eye?

How can I share my piece with others?

What other narrative subjects could I write about?

GLOSSARY

chronological Relating to the order in which something happened.

complex sentence A sentence formed by one independent clause and one or more dependent clauses.

compound sentence A sentence in which two independent clauses are joined with a coordinating conjunction.

conjunction A word used to connect individual words or groups of words.

content The substance of a piece; what is contained in a body of writing.

copyright The exclusive right to the publication of literary and artistic work.

dependent clause A clause that cannot stand on its own and thus depends on the rest of the sentence to make a complete sentence.

dialogue The conversation between characters in a piece of work.

figure of speech A device, such as personification, metaphor, or simile, used by authors to create a special meaning.

flashback A memory of a past experience, often described as a character relives an event that had particular importance in his or her life.

flash forward To move the story ahead, anticipating how a situation may turn out.

foreshadow A warning or clue about something that will happen later in the story.

grammar The guidelines and rules writers follow in order to speak and write in an acceptable manner.

graphics Photos or illustrations used to accompany a written story.

hyperbole Extreme exaggeration or overstatement used for emphasis.

independent clause A clause that expresses a complete thought and can stand alone as a sentence.

inner dialogue A character's thoughts that are presented in a way that reveals the person is talking to himself or herself.

paraphrase The rewording of a spoken passage, while retaining its overall meaning.

plot The plan of action in a story.

point of view The focus of the story from a character's perspective.

proofreading Reviewing the final version of a story for any errors.

sensory details Use of the five senses to describe something.

slang Informal speech.

transition Wording or phrasing that smoothly ties two ideas together.

FOR MORE INFORMATION

Kenyon Review Young Writers Workshop

Finn House

102 West Wiggin Street

Kenyon College

Gambier, OH 43022

(740) 427-5208

Young Writers is an intensive two-week workshop for high school students who value writing. The program is sponsored by the _Kenyon Review_, one of the country's preeminent literary magazines.

National Council of Teachers of English (NCTE)

Achievement Awards in Writing

1111 West Kenyon Road

Urbana, IL 61801-1096

Web site: http://www.ncte.org

The NCTE's Achievement Awards in Writing is a school-based writing program established in 1957 to encourage high school students in their writing and recognize publicly some of the best student writers in the nation.

Scholastic Art & Writing Awards

Alliance for Young Artists & Writers

557 Broadway

New York, NY 10012

Web site: http://www.artandwriting.org

The Alliance for Young Artists & Writers, a nonprofit organization, identifies teenagers with exceptional artistic and literary talent and brings their work to a national audience through the Scholastic Art & Writing Awards.

Weekly Reader Publishing

Weekly Reader's Student Publishing Contest
3001 Cindel Drive
Delran, NJ 08075
(800) 446-3355
Web site: http://www.weeklyreader.com
Weekly Reader's Student Publishing Contest honors the nation's best nonfiction writing by students in grades 3 to 12.

Publishing and Posting

Below is a list of publications and Web sites that welcome submissions from young writers.

Merlyn's Pen

11 South Angell Street, Suite 301
Providence, RI 02906
(800) 247-2027
E-mail:Merlyn@merlynspen.org
Web site: http://www.merlynspen.org

Stone Soup

P.O. Box 83
Santa Cruz, CA 95063
(800) 447-4569

E-mail: editor@stonesoup.com

Web site: http://www.stonesoup.com

TeenInk

P.O. Box 30

Newton, MA 02461

(617) 964-6800

E-mail: editor@teenink.com

Web site: http://www.teenink.com

Teen Voices

80 Summer Street, Suite 300

Boston, MA 02110

(617) 426-5505

E-mail: teenvoices@teenvoices.com

Web site: http://www.teenvoices.com

Web Sites

Due to the changing nature of Internet links, Rosen Publishing has developed an online list of Web sites related to the subject of this book. This site is updated regularly. Please use this link to access the list:

http://www.rosenlinks.com/wlp/wan

FOR FURTHER READING

Benke, Karen. *Rip the Page!: Adventures in Creative Writing*. Boston, MA: Trumpeter Books, 2010.

DiPrince, Dawn, and Cheryl Miller Thurston. *Unjournaling: Daily Writing Exercises That Are NOT Personal, NOT Introspective, NOT Boring!* Fort Collins, CO: Cottonwood Press, 2006.

Elliott, Rebecca S. *Painless Grammar*. Hauppauge, NY: Barron's Educational Series, 2006.

Fogarty, Mignon. *Grammar Girl Presents the Ultimate Writing Guide for Students*. New York, NY: Henry Holt, 2011.

Hanley, Victoria. *Seize the Story: A Handbook for Teens Who Like to Write*. Fort Collins, CO: Cottonwood Press, 2008.

Kellner, Hank. *Write What You See: 99 Photos to Inspire Writing*. Fort Collins, CO: Cottonwood Press, 2009.

Learning Express Editors. *Writing in 15 Minutes a Day: Junior Skill Builder*. New York, NY: Learning Express, 2008.

Prentice Hall. *Prentice Hall Writing and Grammar: Communication in Action*. Upper Saddle River, NJ: Prentice Hall, 2008.

Schwartz, Tina P. *Writing and Publishing: The Ultimate Teen Guide*. Lanham, MD: Scarecrow Press, 2010.

INDEX

About the Authors

Roger Beutel is a writer who lives in Larchmont, New York.

Lauren Spencer is originally from California and now lives in New York City, where she teaches writing workshops in the public schools. She also writes lifestyle and music articles for magazines.

Photo Credits

Cover David Malan/Getty Images; pp. 4–5 Image Source/ Getty Images; pp. 9, 30 Shutterstock.com; pp. 11, 23, 49 © www.istockphoto.com/by_nicholas; p. 27 © www.istockphoto .com/Dori OConnell; p. 33 © Bill Aron/PhotoEdit; pp. 37, 43 © www.istockphoto.com/Viktoriya Yatskina; p. 46 Hill Street Studios/Blend Images/Getty Images; p. 51 Courtesy Stone Soup Magazine, www.stonesoup.com.

Photo Researcher: Karen Huang